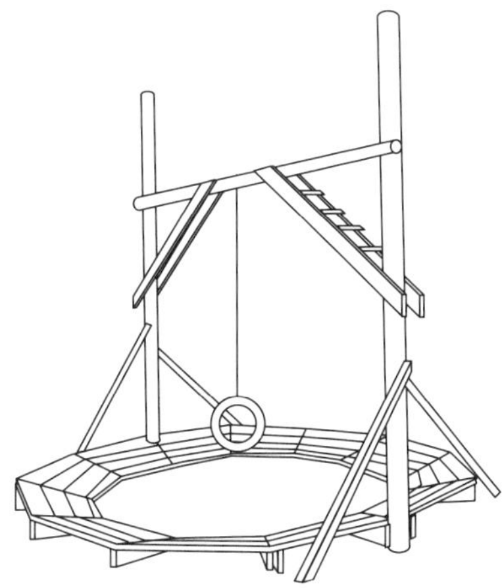

An architecture of play: a survey of London's adventure playgrounds

Nils Norman

for **Séan Kimber** and **Colin de Land**

Photography and drawings by **Nils Norman**

Edited by **Richard Embray** and **Elinor Jansz**

Design by **Tim Barnes**, chicken www.herechickychicky.com

1,000 copies printed in the UK by **Special Blue**

Published by **Four Corners Books**
PO Box 33759, London SW3 4YP
info@fourcornersbooks.co.uk www.fourcornersbooks.co.uk

ISBN **0 9545025 0 7**

Distributed by **art data**
12 Bell Industrial Estate, 50 Cunnington Street, London W4 5HB
t: + 44 (0) 20 8747 1061 f: + 44 (0) 20 8742 2319 orders@artdata.co.uk

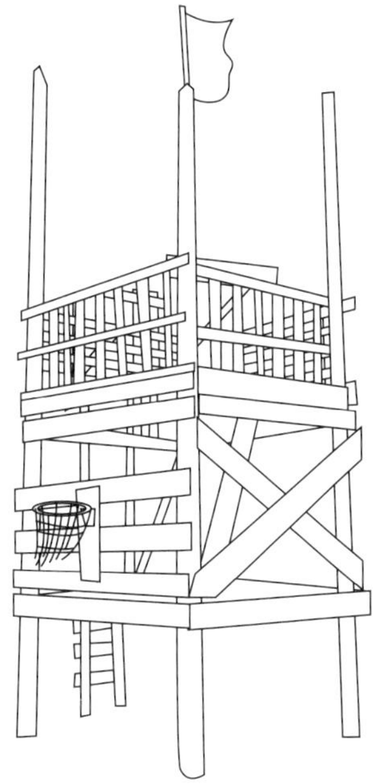

Contents

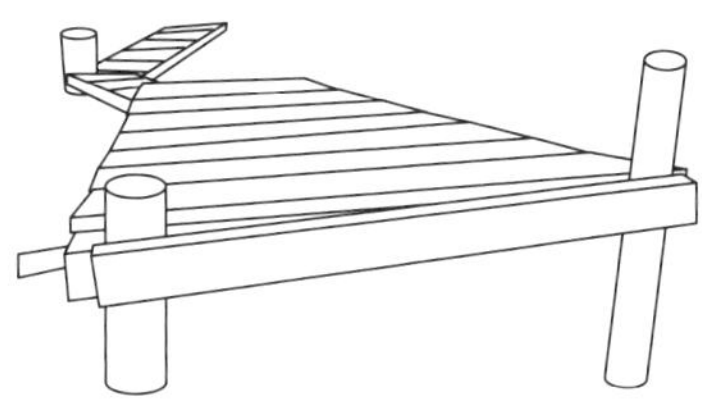

Introduction

It is difficult today to imagine London during the early days of adventure playgrounds after the Second World War. There was a surplus of large open spaces in the form of bombsites, many of which had not been redeveloped even by the 1970s. The earliest playgrounds began as grassroots initiatives on these sites set up by children and their parents. Few playgrounds of this type survive, but in other parts of Europe examples can still be found of these ad hoc playgrounds, full of timber, exposed nails and tool sheds for the children to use. Here, children have designed and built almost all of the structures, the half finished huts, extensive tunnel networks and massive fire pits. Aerial runways double up as makeshift skateboard runs made from cobbled together sheets of plywood. See-saws are like medieval child catapults. This is what the early playgrounds in London must have been like, embodying "the spirit of adventure play", a phrase that evokes a creative, anarchic, children-led playscape.

This free play is the opposite of its municipal cousin, fixed play. Fixed play is the term used to describe the inflexible ironmongery of unattended modular metal climbing frames and swings. They are usually designed not by the users, but by an

Battersea Park, 1975 [p36]

architect, an artist or (worst of all) an urban planner: to put it simply, by a grown-up.

The first adventure playgrounds in Britain were established in the late 1940s and early 1950s and were known as "junk playgrounds". Most of them were set up by unpaid volunteers and parents driven by a strong belief in creating stimulating places for children to play. Following the volunteers' lead, the government and local authorities became more involved in subsequent years.

The majority of London's council-run adventure playgrounds began as Greater London Council initiatives during the 1970s; some were also set up by local parents as voluntary operations that were often later taken over by the council. Today, the remaining independent voluntary sector playgrounds, some of which are affiliated to local councils and/or receive partial funding from them, operate under the leadership of voluntary management committees.

Whether council or volunteer-managed, many playgrounds still have an energetic and creative character, thanks to the efforts and long term commitments of the playworkers who run them. But the slow drain of resources, coupled with stricter health and safety regulations, has made the job of all playworkers more difficult. Many playworkers have expressed their frustration that they are moving away from actual playwork to being full-time fundraisers.

There are currently 14 London Play Associations in London, each affiliated to a different borough. LPAs are dynamic voluntary organisations, often working directly with children, designing and building playgrounds with them, training playworkers, lobbying politicians and council departments, representing community-run play projects and sitting on official steering groups. Only Hackney Play Association has a design and build team, trained to consult with children and realise their designs as playstructures, but there are hopes that a London-wide team will soon be established. Another independent organisation, London Play, now in its fifth year, has been instrumental in promoting play across the capital and establishing new Play Associations.

While adventure playgrounds evolved out of local children making good use of derelict spaces after the Blitz, today the playgrounds themselves seem to be as vulnerable as the bombsites once were: they occupy highly sought-after land, making their sites incredibly valuable. Three Corners, for example, is a large open space in Clerkenwell, one of the most highly inflated speculative property markets in Europe. The playgrounds themselves are in a state of constant un-development which contrasts with the frenzied development taking place around them. The playground allows for diverse groups of children to meet and play, facilitating integration among different economic and ethnic backgrounds: adventure playgrounds today remain models for a totally radical and extremely valuable form of public space.

previous page Deptford [p38] **above** tunnel, Weavers [p61];
below cantilevered swing, The Dumps [p39]

above musical instrument, ELHAP [p40]; communications system, Rockingham [p56]
below slide, Harebreaks, Watford; bowling alley, Homerton [p42]

clockwise from left sensory room, Acklam Playspace [p34]; Stop The War banner, Palace [p48]; entry sign, Marble Hill [p47]

clockwise from above
fixed play; view from a tower, Bethwin Road [p36]; children's den, King Henry's Walk [p44]

above The Rec, Ripon Street, Sheffield, 1972
below Weavers, 1976 [p61]

photo: Jess Milne

Towards a history of adventure playgrounds 1931–2000

Keith Cranwell

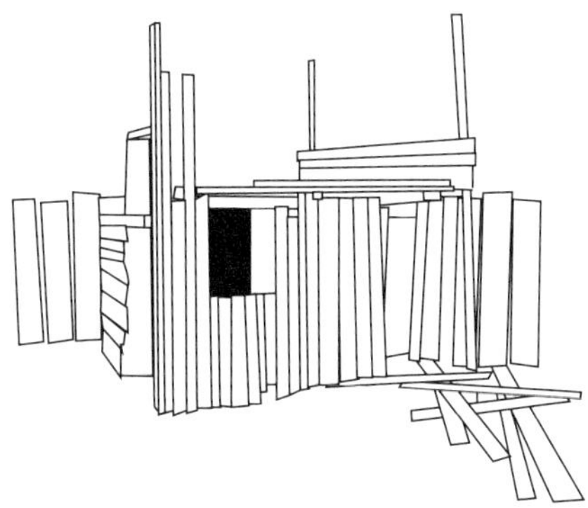

The Beginning of an Idea – Liberation (1931–1948)

In 1931, the Danish architect and landscape designer C T Sørenson first mentioned "junk" playgrounds in his book *Open Spaces for Town and Country*. Adventure playground pioneer Joe Benjamin[1] suggests Sørenson's concept arose from his observation of children playing on building sites after the workers had finished for the day. This pragmatic solution gave rise to a revolutionary idea that transformed the play landscape of children in the city.

On the 15th of August 1943 at Emdrupvej, on the outskirts of Copenhagen, the first junk playground was opened under the leadership of John Bertelsen and enabled by M Dan Fink, architect to the Workers' Cooperative Housing Association. Denmark was then under German occupation and the need for a place for children to play arose from the moral confusion under occupation when small acts of childhood delinquency could be interpreted as sabotage and severely punished. Indeed, the playground site at Emdrupvej was hidden from view by a six-foot bank topped by a fence, as if children's play represented some form of rebellion to occupation and needed to be hidden. The children improvised their dens and earth caves from bricks, boards, fir-posts and cement pillars using a variety of tools including wheelbarrows, spades, hammers and nails.

The difficulties for the playground did not cease with the end of the occupation, and there was trouble from the Danish local authorities when in 1947 the children built a tower that was higher than the bank that hid the playground. Bertelsen attempted to defend the children's right to build and construct their own vision of the world but it was clear that the Housing Association wanted him to take charge and organise games for children. This attempt to impose activities upon children, Bertelsen felt, cut across the original intentions of the playground as a place where "children are themselves the creators"[2], putting conditions upon his work that were unacceptable, and he resigned.

Bertelsen is important not just as the leader of the first "junk playground" but for inspiring Sørenson's playground concept. For Bertelsen the playground was much more than a physical environment where children could play with waste materials – it was a psychical space for children's imagination and creativity. Bertelsen's view was that to accompany a "pro-child" physical environment there needed to be a "pro-play" psychical background. The task that faced the pioneers of the adventure play movement was to educate adults to understand the meaning of being "pro-play" on sites that to the outward gaze were dirty and messy pieces of scrap land.

Regeneration (1948–1956)

In 1946 whilst on a British Council lecture tour to Norway, Lady Allen of Hurtwood[3], had a stopover in Copenhagen when she visited the Emdrupvej playground, and wrote about it for *Picture Post*. What impressed Lady Allen was the wealth of play opportunities that waste materials provided and the lack of man-made play equipment. She felt that the activities of digging, den-building, experimentation with sand, water or fire under the benign eye of a playleader enabled children to learn about responsibility through the freedom of play.

In Lady's Allen's view, the junk playground was a place where children could experiment, be encouraged to build and create their own space away from the street. The playground would be an environment that had endless possibilities and could never be considered immutable, unlike those with man-made fixed equipment. In her view, the adventure playground had three functions: to recreate the kinds of play that adults had enjoyed in their own childhoods, to answer critics who felt that children's use of their free time was "empty and purposeless", and to meet the needs of children who "do not enjoy organised games, playground asphalt and mechanical swings."[4]

In 1948, with support from the Under-14s Committee and the Cambridge House Settlement, London's first official junk playground opened in Camberwell.[5] For three years this playground thrived as the St Luke's or Rosemary Junk

Playground, until the land was needed for redevelopment. In 1951, Lady Allen joined another venture that established the Clydesdale Playground in Kensington. Meanwhile, other junk playgrounds had begun to establish themselves as isolated experiments set up by enthusiastic local people whose only resource tended to be time coupled with a passion for this form of children's play. Often the land available could only be used for a short time prior to development and there were no grants to equip and run these projects.[6] It was clear that if a playground movement was to gather momentum then it needed support from a national body.

In 1953 Lord Luke, Chair of the National Playing Fields Association (NPFA) called a meeting to explore the development of junk playgrounds. At this time, the main purpose of the NPFA was to promote children's playgrounds and playing fields. Achieving recognition from this national charitable body was a significant step forward for individual playgrounds like the Clydesdale playground, which received a capital grant, and for the promotion of waste material playgrounds more generally. However, the term "junk" was felt to be a drawback to gaining local authority funding and needed to be changed. Sir George Pepler and Lady Allen came up with the idea of calling them adventure playgrounds.[7]

The word "adventure" linked the playground with the ideals of the newly created Outward Bound Trust (founded in 1946), which provided young people with opportunities to undertake healthy outdoor activities and challenges thereby providing an important shift towards the importance of adult leadership. The term was more robust and, according to Drummond Abernethy, who was head of the Children's Play Department at the NPFA from 1956–1977, more readily suggested to children that these play environments could be places that "transfer the attractions of the streets – light, colour, movement, sound, excitement and a sense of danger – to a playground".[8]

Playleadership 1956–1964

The adventure playground was perceived as a "supplement" to parks, playgrounds, play centres and playing fields – "a means of supplying the vitamins to the child's inadequate recreational diet".[9] Moreover, behind this idea was the expectation that the adventure play experiment would make the "old-fashioned playgrounds of fixed equipment on a sea of asphalt ... relics of the past"[10] as the value of the work began to be recognised.

Between 1948–1960 seventeen playgrounds were established in areas as diverse as new towns (Crawley, 1954), Grimsby (1955) and Liverpool (1956) and several in London, the most notable being Lollard Street (1956). In 1956, Drummond Abernethy was appointed to the NPFA with a brief to promote playleadership and adventure playgrounds nationally[11] and by 1971 the NPFA had a team of seven Regional Officers supporting the NPFA's role to establish the standards for adventure playgrounds.

In its pamphlet "What is an Adventure Playground", the NPFA set out a vision of adventure play that identified play activities, access for all children, playleader supervision, the model management structure, equipment, landscaping and indoor accommodation, 'The Play Hut'. This was often little more than a wooden Nissen hut with some storage, space for indoor crafts, an office for the playworker, a rudimentary kitchen and sometimes easy chairs or an old sofa[12]. The pamphlet emphasised the importance of the community in maintaining the success of the playground. Abernethy's view of adventure playgrounds was that they were the "hub of the community". By this he meant that the playground

> "must be part of the whole community and be involved in every aspect of the life of the people making the community. It is not a separate entity, nor is it in competition with the Youth Service; rather the playleader is cooperating with all leaders, teachers and parents and is a friend and helper of all children, teenagers and tiny tots".[13]

Yet, despite the great energy behind the movement, by 1960 adventure playgrounds were still mostly short-term experiments based on inadequately protected sites and unsuitable pieces of land, sometimes having only sufficient funding for part-time provision. What had been learnt from the few pioneer playgrounds was that the whole process of acquiring land for a site, creating a management group to administer, support and fund the playground was a complex community development process requiring specialist workers to carry the task forward. Moreover, where playgrounds were most successful they tended to be administered by local authorities.

It was during this period that the playleader employed to supervise the playground was established as a key figure and took over the responsibilities formerly covered by local volunteers. In the 1960s and 1970s the ideal playleader was someone who embraced the work as a way of life "demanding an almost limitless talent for human relationships, judgment, perception administrative ability, a good and respected character and enormous physical toughness and stamina."[14] The emphasis was on the individual's personal qualities rather than qualifications[15] that made them technicians in playground management. It was little wonder that "burn out" was frequent; the average working life of a playleader in this period being estimated as six to nine months.

The Rec, Ripon Street, Sheffield, 1971–4 photos: Jess Milne

Community solutions (1964–1987)

Adventure playgrounds provided a unique centre of support in the community partly because they were able to cater to children of all ages[16]. The under fives child care provision attached to some adventure playgrounds made up for the shortage of day nursery provision. For example, Pat Turner, after his work as leader of the Lollard Street playground, developed "The One O'clock Under Fives" for the Greater London Council. Activities taking place in playgrounds strengthened the networking function to bring social groups together from toddler groups to pensioners' tea parties and encouraged a supportive atmosphere where children undertook community service tasks such as wood deliveries to pensioners, while parents would donate waste material or rally round in a crisis.

Since the activities of adventure playgrounds were located at the heart of the community they were inevitably involved in local politics. In 1976, an article in a national newspaper accused Islington playground workers of political indoctrination for attending a council-funded three-day course called "Political Education and Young People" which looked at the issue of political illiteracy among children covering topics such as racism, unemployment, powerlessness and sexism. Around this time the press accused playworkers of offending a local Conservative MP by taking children to a "Rock Against Racism" event rather than attend a prize-giving event at which he was a guest; using camping trips to spread left wing propaganda and opposing an attempt by the National Front to remove a "foreign" playworker from the playground where they worked.

Between 1960 and the 1980s adventure playgrounds benefited from programmes that supported child–centred active learning (the Plowden Report and Educational Priority Areas), urban regeneration (Community Development Projects), inner city poverty (Urban Programme 1968–1987) and job creation programmes. In 1972 Bernard McGovern, play manager in the London Borough of Lewisham, distanced himself from these aims by criticising the view that the playworker should have a high profile role in the community. He felt that a community liaison responsibility detracted from the main task of providing playground activities and led to the perpetuation of a fear that adventure playgrounds were full of juvenile delinquents. This misconception was partly rooted in the fact that the justification for setting up an adventure playground was often promoted as a way to decrease crime in the area or the only way to reach the "unattached" or disaffected youth.

In 1985 there were 189 local authority run adventure playgrounds and approximately 15–20 voluntary playgrounds[17]. In 1970, Lady Allen had created the first playground for disabled children on a site provided by the Bishop of London in the grounds of the Old Rectory, Chelsea. From this work grew HAPA, an organisation promoting other playgrounds for disabled children. Renamed Kidsactive in 1999, in 2003 it merged with the national disabled children's charity KIDS, supporting seven London playgrounds designed primarily for disabled children.

Retrenchment (1987–2000)

In 1984 the government created the Playboard, a quango, with the purpose of bringing children's play interests under one umbrella organisation to provide expertise to enable local bodies to create meaningful local policies for children's out-of-school leisure.

Now one umbrella organisation could plan children's play interests through research, strengthening regional provision to provide expertise to local bodies, formulating national standards for playwork training and an accessible information service. Within three years much of the promise of the organisation to generate new funding for play, particularly through the private sector, led to the government to seek to merge Playboard with the Sports Council. The Playboard directors, who saw the merger as cutting the level of services available to support children's play through having a smaller head office team, rejected this development and decided that rather than merge with the Sports Council they would wind up Playboard. The acrimonious winding up of Playboard, its reorganisation as the Children's Play and Recreation Unit and the return of children's play to NPFA in 1990 meant that adventure play no longer had a credible national lobby that could protect its fragile inheritance.

At a local level, the interpretation of the 1974 Health and Safety Act gave local authorities an opportunity to question the place of untidy and messy sites where children used a range of tools and materials that were potentially dangerous and expensive to defend litigiously[18]. In 1987 the loss of Urban Programme funding meant local authorities had to find the full costs of playgrounds in a period when all local authority expenditure was being cut. The 1989 Children's Act development of Child Protection Policy meant that the free "come and go" access, on which the adventure playground ethos rested, was more formally monitored with tighter control over children's use of the provision. The 1998 launch of the National Childcare Strategy, placed the emphasis on the care of the child, undertaking purposeful play activities, as a paid "out-of-school" service which required that children be registered with a playground and only allowed to leave under strict supervision of a carer. This has created a situation on some adventure playgrounds where one group of children are "open access" and free to leave and return to the playground as they wish, alongside children who cannot leave without a recognised carer – creating two types playground user. It remains to be seen whether the community-based adventure playground with a strong identification with the locality can withstand the incursions of a system that rests on payment for care rather than free access to a creative play environment based on the equality of a child's right to enjoy the playground.[19]

The adventure playground is a model of counter-urbanisation. According to D N Lord the way we organise our lives and the lives of our children in the inner city denies us a physical space "so that we are forever queuing, walking in crowds, jostling for tubes or buses, bumping into, trying to avoid bumping into, other people", and equally, modern city life denies us psychic space. The hope is that once we understand the effects of these pressures on us as adults and recognise the effects this has on children then we might rediscover the simple message that Bertelsen gave us from Emdrupvej to rediscover the pro-child physical space and the pro-play psychical space.

Notes

1 Joe Benjamin was a local authority play manager and play educationalist.

2 Bengtsson, p20

3 Marjorie Allen (1898–1976) was a landscape architect, gardener and children's advocate for causes as diverse as nursery schools, early childhood education (OMEP), children's cinema clubs, homeless children and adventure playgrounds for the disabled.

4 Allen, 1953, pp1–3

5 Joe Benjamin, 1974, p12 and Ray Wills, in an unpublished manuscript, suggest that an earlier playground existed in Morden, Surrey.

6 The 1944 Education Act, Section 53 gave local authorities powers to provide facilities for children's leisure but was rarely used either in this period or subsequently. (E J Beattie, *Playtimes*, Issue 15, May 1979, p12)

7 Joe Benjamin, 1974, p25, suggests another, earlier origin of the term.

8 Abernethy, "Playleadership", 1967, p391

9 Mays, 1957, p6

10 Allen, 1975, p55

11 Drummond Abernethy (1913–1988). Former teacher, worked for the Educational division of the Rank organisation and was Secretary to the International Playground Association (1963–1972). He worked for NPFA from 1956–1977 where he was head of the Children's Play Department. He was also a member of numerous national and governmental youth initiatives.

12 The first NPFA pamphlets covered health and safety issues, equipment and provision of play buildings ('the Hut'). These became the foundation of a basic safety checklist written by Tony Chilton and Bill McCulloch.

13 Abernethy, 1967, p13

14 Keenan, M, 1967

15 In 1970 the NPFA sponsored the first full-time training for playworkers at Thurrock Technical College.

16 Records of age groups on playgrounds in the 1980s show much local variation, ranging between 2–20 and 6–18.

17 *London Evening Standard*, July 18th 1976, p8; *Daily Telegraph* (undated), Playlink/LAPA archive. *Playtimes*, September 1978, recorded that there were 260 adventure playgrounds, 160 out of London.

18 1980s reports on playground safety revealed fewer, less serious accidents reported on adventure playground than on unsupervised playgrounds.

19 Bengtsson, 1972, p2

Bibliography

Abernethy, D, "Playleadership" in Leicester, J H, *Trends in the Services for Youth*, Pergamon Press, Oxford, 1967, pp390–393

Abernethy, D, *Recreation and Play*, 3rd Triennial Conference of the International Playground Association, 1967

Abernethy, D, *Playleadership – its significance for the "unattached"*, NPFA, undated

Allen, M, *Adventure Playgrounds*, NPFA, London, 1953

Allen, M, *Planning for Play*, Thames and Hudson, London, 1975

Allen, M, and Nicholson, M, *Memoirs of an Uneducated Lady*, Thames and Hudson, London, 1975

Bengtsson, A, *Adventure Playgrounds*, Crosby Lockwood, London, 1972

Benjamin, J, *Grounds for Play*, Bedford Square Press, London, 1974

Benjamin, J, "Play and Participation" in *Streetwise*, No. 2, Autumn 1992, pp2–8

Buck, D, *Report on the Relevance of an Adventure Playground to the Study and Control of Juvenile Delinquency*, unpublished, Children's Play Information Centre, 1965

Chance, M (ed), *The Provision for Children's Play*, 1983

Danby, S, *Big Hill Adventure Playground*, NPFA, London, 1977

Heseltine, P, "Failing to Communicate Play" in Hughes, B (ed), *Play Ed 1982 – The Transcripts*, Play Education, Ely, 1982

Hughes, B, "Notes For Adventure Playworkers", CYAG, 1980, p31

Keenan, M, "Follow My Leader", Sunday Times 16th April 1967

Lord, D N, *Calling in the Country: Ecology, Parks and Human Needs*, Comedia, Gloucester, 1994

McGovern, letter in *Playrights*, No. 1., May 1972, p29

Mays, J B, *Adventure in Play: The Story of Rathbone Street Adventure Playground*, Liverpool Council of Social Service, Liverpool, 1957

Murofushi, K, *A Thinking of Play: A Japanese Playworker's Views of Adventure Playgrounds in Britain*, unpublished Associateship Study, Institute of Education, London, 1987

O'Malley, *The Politics of Community Action*, Spokesman, Nottingham, 1977

Research Institute for Consumer Affairs, *Children's Playgrounds*, 1982

Rojek, C, "Leisure Time and Leisure Space", pp191–203 in Rojek, C (ed), *Leisure for Leisure*, Macmillan, London, 1989

Turner, H S, *Something Extraordinary*, Michael Joseph, London, 1961

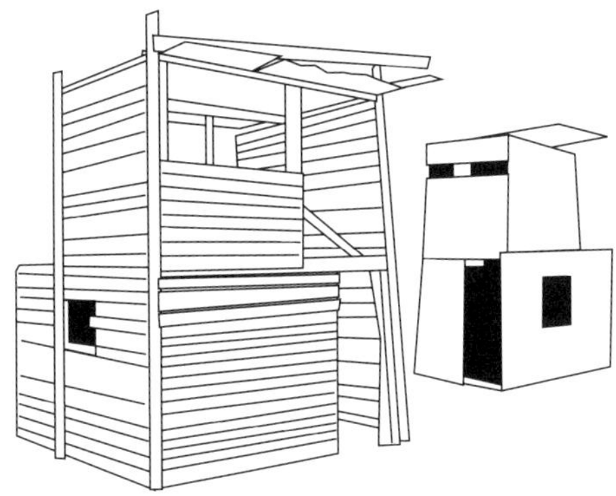

The vernacular of play
Paul Claydon

"...one of the most important characters of play was its spatial separation from ordinary life. A closed space is marked out for it either materially or ideally, hedged off from the everyday surroundings. Inside this space the play proceeds, inside it the rules obtain." **Jan Huizinga**[1]

"As a genius of construction man raises himself far above the bee in the following way, whereas the bee builds with wax that she gathers from nature, man builds with the far more delicate conceptual material which he first has to manufacture from himself." **Friedrich Nietzsche**[2]

The overwhelming sovereignty of play renders all architecture, to a greater or lesser degree, an arena for play, and throughout history children have found the means to employ the fabric of the city for their games and entertainments. But the changing character of the city and its streets in our own time, the widespread fears for children's safety and the acknowledgement of their needs as distinct from adults, set in motion the provision of children's own spaces within the city.

Aerial tunnel and pyramid, Battersea Park, 1973 [p360] photo: Jumbo

From a historical perspective, the development of the urban adventure playground, from its post-war origins to the present day, can be considered as an exercise in problem solving. As a rule the projects are initiated in deprived or heavily built up urban areas where before there was little alternative to playing in the street. At least in the beginning this was recognised not by government but by individuals with almost no financial means, who often appropriated land and built structures without official permission or co-operation.

Early experiments in the field are described in John Barron Mays' 1951 book *Adventure in Play*[3] and owed much to the possibilities offered by the wide-open spaces created by the devastation of aerial bombardment during the Second World War. Improvised structures were built using waste materials such as sewer pipes, reclaimed masonry, old boats, railway sleepers and oil drums. In 1972 Arvid Bengtsson's book *Adventure Playgrounds*[4] suggested models that were more structured and enclosed, mimetic in nature like miniature villages, a forest of wooden towers and Wendy houses. Earlier American experiments at The Yard in Minneapolis showed that when left to their own initiative, children were indeed inclined to build shelters, converting 10,000 feet of used timber into shacks in a matter of days.

But each innovation brings with it its own particular problems. Surveillance and supervision, for instance, are difficult to maintain with so many enclosed spaces, and this can lead to accidents which ultimately attract the attention of

exterior bodies such as the health and safety executive. This in turn can limit the possibilities of adventure playgrounds through the direct intervention of unwarranted legislation. The mould for most modern playgrounds is a more or less open network of brightly painted ramps and towers connected by ladders and slides of various kinds. Variety, such as the introduction of baking ovens, or the consultation and co-operation of the children in matters of design, is an ongoing facet of the innovation of individual playgrounds but they also share a great deal in common.

These spaces take on a political aspect because not only do they provide a solution to the lack of supervised and engaging places for children to play, they also represent a defiance of the proscriptive oppression and indifference of the modern built environment. The conceptual structures of play, and by extension its physical structures, are continuously generating and degenerating and peculiar to the particular and perishable rules, circumstances and impulses of the participants. These phenomena are similar to the constantly fluctuating dialects and uses of vernacular language which at once help to change and shape verbal communication and which, like play, will always undermine the imposition of a rigid canonical order.

Seen within an architectural canon, adventure playgrounds are a microcosmic distillation of the playful possibilities of architecture, or a vernacular of play. This vernacular spirit arises from a community's resolution to find solutions to some quite specific problems within an exclusive built environment. On a functional level, the adventure playground is simply a co-operative venture to provide a contained area for children to play. Moreover, and almost without exception, this definition can be examined in relation to encouraging both the vertiginous and the mimetic aspects of children's play.

By far the more prevalent of the two forms found in modern playgrounds is the vertiginous aspect which is effected by the introduction of physical challenge, height, speed, motion and, it follows, the element of risk. Roger Caillois, in his book, *Man, Play and Games,*[5] describes it as the most primal aspect of play:

> "...an attempt to momentarily destroy the stability of perception and inflict a kind of voluptuous panic on an otherwise lucid mind... Surrendering to a kind of spasm, seizure or shock which destroys reality with sovereign brusqueness."

Towers, bridges, catwalks and an aerial runway, Slade Gardens, 1984 [p58] photo: Jumbo

In every event this factor is controlled either by the architecture itself (railings, nets or crash mats) or by supervision by playworkers or parents. Despite its less dangerous characteristics, however, the mimetic factor is far more problematic. There is a danger of limiting the extent to which imaginative play can be realised by over-emphasising the thematic structure of a space; a square enclosure can be imagined as a number of different environments: add battlements, turrets or a drawbridge and it immediately becomes more exclusive. The site of play must simultaneously maintain the vertiginous and mimetic elements, without obliterating the neutrality of the space which allows the child to joyfully pursue her own imagination, which Caillois describes as Paidia. For that reason the action of this kind of architecture has to be more "methectic rather than mimetic", that is, more "a helping-out of the action" than a proscription of its likely character.

Superficially, the sports arena begs comparison as its simplicity lends itself to any number of agonistic athletic contests, but that is where the similarity ends. Lewis Mumford, in *Technics and Civilization*[6] writes that

> "unlike play, mass sport usually requires an element of mortal chance or hazard as one of its main ingredients: but instead of chances occurring spontaneously as in mountain climbing, it must take place within the rules of the game and must be increased when the spectacle bores the spectators."

It would be a mistake to imagine that there can be any further connections between the institutions that govern the various sporting bodies and the children who lay out their coats and bags to designate a football pitch, but the games that stem from play are ultimately its bridge to the exterior world. For as Roger Caillois points out:

> "Rules are inescapable from play once the latter has become institutionalised. From this moment on they become part of its nature. They transform it into an instrument of fecund and decisive culture. But a basic freedom is central to play in order to stimulate distraction and fantasy. This liberty is its indispensable motive power."

Children's play, then, is contradictory; it can happen spontaneously in any given environment, its specific location being only a nominal contributing factor to the acting-out of play. It is usually self generated, and unlike sport, unregulated by external bodies and proceeding for the most part without audience. And yet, once the play commences the strict rules that must necessarily apply in order to maintain the illusion that separates play from reality become as unforgiving and as 'four-square' as a prison yard. Johan Huizinga in his seminal work, *Homo Ludens*, sees this as one of the main characteristics of play, 'its secludedness, its limitedness. It is "played out" within certain limits of time and space. It contains its own course and meaning'. In order for that hermetic space to be maintained one must abide by the rules of the game: "They determine what 'holds' in the temporary world circumscribed by play. The rules of the game are absolutely binding and allow no doubt". Huizinga also highlights the importance of the physical parameters of play:

> "More striking even than the limitation as to time is the limitation as to space. All play moves and has its being within a playground marked off beforehand either materially or ideally, deliberately or as a matter of course."

The delicate conceptual fabric of the illusion depends on a stronger structure to support it and explains the seemingly anomalous introduction of rules into the arena of free play. Even the word illusion has its origins in the Latin word for play or, as Caillois stresses, "means nothing less than beginning a game: *in lusio*".

Illusion encloses the conceptual space of play, furnishing it with all the unique specialisations needed for the play to be acted out. It is tempting to see the desire to enclose or limit the space of play as an architectonic drive. But if so, then it is no more than a further support to play. Like its physical counterpart, the play-structure, the illusion must behave somewhat like the outer skein of a tent, held rigid by the poles, the rules of the game, which in turn help to enclose the action. A vital yet contingent series of layers, it serves merely to preserve the action of play from contamination.

The physical framework within which play takes place does not direct it as such – the playground is not instilled with meaning but rather changes its character from one game to the next, rendered only by the sovereignty of play. At best, it is more a methectic vehicle than a building. And a vehicle, moreover, in which all kinetic activity is directed inward.

This inward drive denudes the play-structure of the physical hallmarks of its use. What is left when the play moves on, when the children have left, is not architecture at all but more like an engine in abeyance, subservient to the action that drives it: the stuff of civil engineers or stage designers, a series of turrets, ropes, ramps and caissons providing an effective space for play. The playground has a specialised external surface, but it becomes a complex space only once it is affected, that is to say, specified by play, for it is only from within ourselves that the accent of play prevails, the *deus ex machina* introduced.

Notes

1 Huizinga, J, *Homo Ludens,* Paladin, London, 1971

2 Nietzsche, F, *Twilight of the Idols and the Antichrist,* trans. R J Hollingdale, Penguin, London, 1968

3 Mays, J B, *Adventure in Play: The Story of Rathbone Street Adventure Playground,* Liverpool Council of Social Service, Liverpool, 1957

4 Bengtsson, A, *Adventure Playgrounds*, Crosby Lockwood, London, 1972

5 Caillois, R, *Man, Play and Games*, University of Illinois Press, Illinois, 2001

6 Mumford, L, *Technics and Civilization*, Routledge & Kegan Paul, London, 1934

London's adventure playgrounds

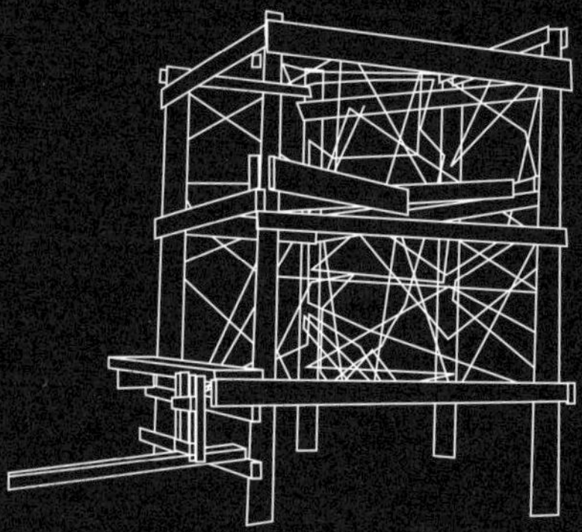

Acklam Playspace

Kensington & Chelsea London W10 [p12]

Hidden under the Westway, Acklam Playspace occupies a two storey building with three outdoor areas.

The facilities include sensory rooms using music, projected patterns and other light effects that enable users to 'tune' the room. All the play structures are under the roof of the Westway. The cars and lorries which can be heard and felt thundering overhead and the tube running directly beside it make this the most futuristic of urban playgrounds.

Set up in 1969 as Acklam Adventure Playground, in 2000 it became Acklam Playspace, run by Kidsactive (see Charlie Chaplin p37).

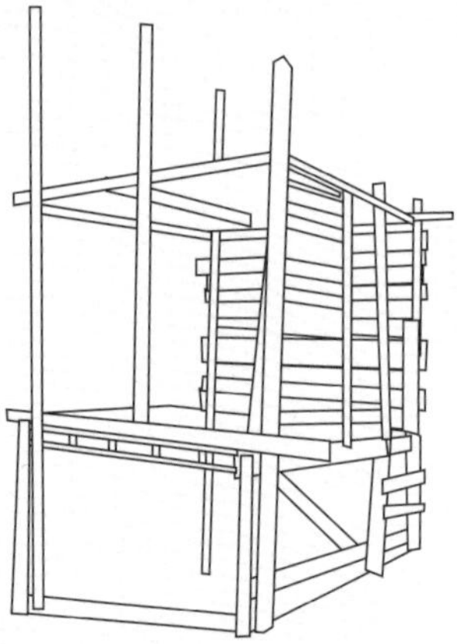

Apples and Pears' Play Association

Hackney London E2

Apples and Pears' was started in 1977 by local mothers as a voluntary run playgroup: a solution to the lack of play facilities in such a densely built-up area. They organised playschemes and camping breaks during school holidays.

In 1983 Hackney Council agreed to fund a consultation worker, with whose help the residents chose a site whose existing prefab houses were ready for demolition. The St. Mary's Garden Group was established and, together with Apples and Pears', applied to lease the land from Hackney Council, who also help provide most funding.

Ashburnham Adventure Playground
Kensington & Chelsea London SW10

This playground began life indoors in a disused factory adjacent to the current site and was known as the "inside-out building".

It was later established outside on an old bombsite. The structures are designed and made together with the children that use them.

Attlee Youth and Community Centre
Tower Hamlets London E1

The playground was established in 1980 as part of the new estate just off Brick Lane.

The playground is protected by a wooden stockade perimeter fence but most of the structures inside have been burnt down and trees and bushes have been removed to prevent drug activity; only the original aerial runway is still standing. Its struggle to survive highlights the crucial role of playgrounds which can provide some children with the only safe place they can play.

An interesting feature of the playground is a reclaimed street that runs through it.

Barnard Park Adventure Playground
Islington London N1

The playground was started in the mid 1970s. Purpose built by the council on demolished housing this is possibly the fifth construction of the present design.

The initial structures were built with help from children using materials from demolition sites and telegraph poles, setting a record for erecting 18 poles in one day. The playground is slightly altered every year and is distinctive in its extensive use of high walkways and ramps.

Battersea Park Adventure Playground
Wandsworth London SW11 [pp6, 26]

Battersea Park Adventure Playground was started by the GLC in the early 1960s on the site of a former barrage balloon station.

The playground had many experimental structures that have now been removed, but it still has some unusual features – such as the tyre tunnels and a very old Tintin-style red rocket.

The playground is now run by Wandsworth Council.

Bethwin Road Adventure Playground
Southwark London SE5 [p15]

Bethwin Road is a small playground with a grassed area and a mound with a handpainted tower.

Lady Allen, in particular, was enthusiastic about play mounds, arguing that an unlevel surface was more exciting and fun for the children who used the playground.

There are also two border swings and an American swing.

Burgess Park Adventure Playground
Southwark London SE5

The playground was moved to its present site in Burgess Park in 1995. Its previous site next door had a classic raised earth bank which can still be seen and has been left to grow wild.

In Victorian times a menagerie occupied this site and it is said that the first giraffe in Britain was exhibited there.

Charlie Chaplin Adventure Playground

Lambeth London SE5

Run by Kidsactive, this award-winning playground was started in 1982 with money donated by Charlie Chaplin's widow Oona Chaplin.

Kidsactive, the leading charity for inclusive play, is now a division of the national charity KIDS and supports seven playgrounds in London, including one in the Royal Hospital Gardens that has to be removed each year for the Chelsea Flower Show. As in all adventure playgrounds, but particularly at Chelsea, where there are few physical structures, energetic and dedicated playworkers who are able to establish relationships with children are key to creating an exciting play environment.

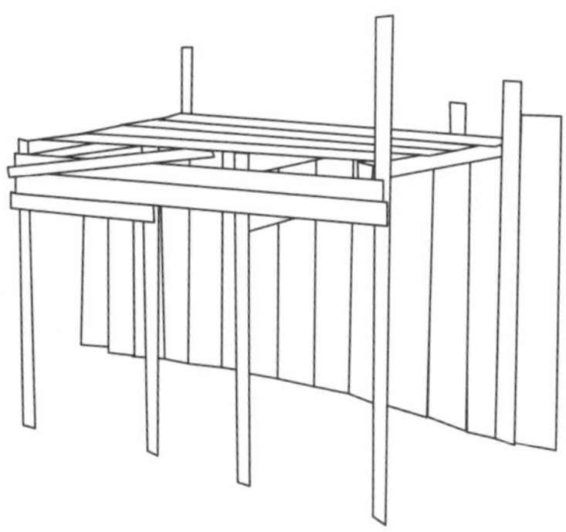

Cornwallis Adventure Playground

Islington London N19

Built on the site of an older adventure playground, Cornwallis is designed by children with structures that keep them off the ground as much as possible.

Temporary structures, dens and camps are attached to the main structure every year and subsequently adapted and removed.

Crumbles Castle Adventure Playground

Islington London N1

Crumbles Castle was built in 1970 by a group of local residents with help from architecture students. Called Crumbles because of the crumbling estate that was there before, the "castle" is the main office and activity centre and has been designed so that its roof is also part of the playscape. The tower is called "The Mushroom" and hides a metal chimney.

Unusually for a London adventure playground, it has a wood yard and tool bank for kids to use and build structures with.

Close consultation with children on designs and structure-building is essential to the character of this imaginative and popular playground.

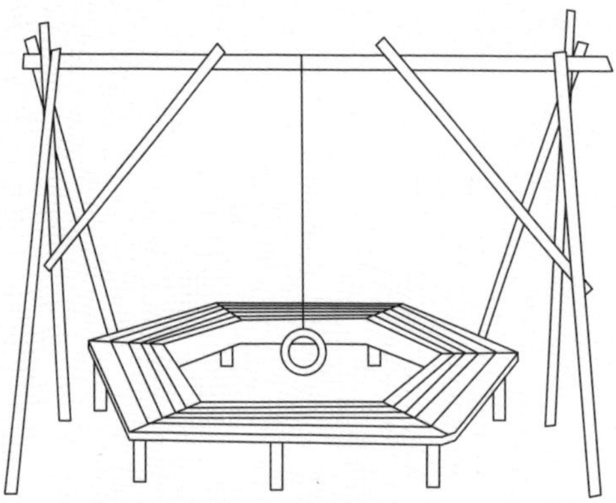

Deptford Adventure Playground

Lewisham London SE8 [p9]

Until the late 1880s the site was occupied by a slaughterhouse. In the 1920s it became Kentish Creamia Dairies which was destroyed during the Second World War. In 1963 the GLC set up the Deptford Adventure Playground. Old milk bottle tops from the dairy can still be found when digging.

Possessing some of the tallest play structures in London, a complex network of three-tiered walkways is packed into an empty lot between buildings, with trees and bushes growing between and around platforms and bridges. The high build is mitigated by platforms that ensure that no fall is greater than seven feet.

Dog Kennel Hill Adventure Playground

Southwark London SE22

Very little of the history of this award-winning playground is known. Started by local residents in the 1970s, it was run by a committee until a fire in 1998. For a short period it was run by Southwark council and is now back in the hands of the voluntary sector.

The playground is situated on a sliver of land halfway up Dog Kennel Hill, overlooking a supermarket. The structures weave in and out of woodland and some even incorporate trees.

The Dumps Adventure Playground

Lewisham London SE4 [p10]

The Dumps was opened in 1975 and is named after the council dump that previously occupied the site. After the council stopped using it, local parents cut a hole in the fence and occupied the site and after many protests claimed it as an adventure playground. Folklore has it that the site was once a graveyard.

The Dumps is one of a few adventure playgrounds in London that keeps chickens, rabbits and hamsters.

ELHAP Adventure Playground

Redbridge London IG8 [p11]

Set up by Drummond Abernethy, ELHAP took over the site from Barnardo's in 1975 and in 1977 it officially opened as a playground for disabled children.

The playground is set in four acres of an old farm; the walls of the farm buildings and traces of an old orchard remain. Two acres are dedicated to a playscape and the remainder left as a nature area with paths and benches. There is also a see-saw that can accommodate wheelchairs.

Pictured is what is left of a "wild west town", one of the earliest features of the playground.

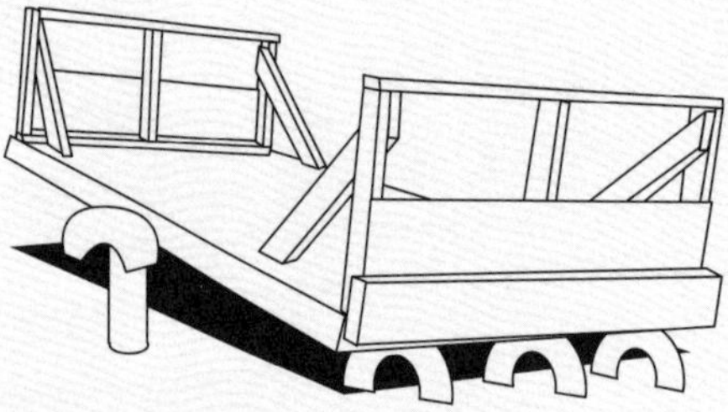

Evergreen Play Association

Hackney London E8

Built on a former wasteground and stonemason's hut in the early 1970s, the playground was set up by local parents and is still in the voluntary sector.

The site used to be flat but there are now a variety of areas including mounds, a small wooded zone and a garden. A children's committee was formed to gather ideas for the playground, mapping pathways and working with architects to plan treehouses and other adventure play structures. There is now a Skyden, a Rocket and an aerial runway. Bees are kept at the playground and their honey sold locally.

As of 2002 Evergreen has been fully integrated for disabled children.

Fredericks Adventure Playground

Southwark London SE17

In 1982 Fredericks was set up by local residents on a former bombsite, and is a very efficient design, using up all available space in a compact corner lot between terraced housing.

It also has a Demon swing that creates an interesting direction change to the usual swinging movement. Some structures are a hybrid of fixed and adventure play.

Glamis Adventure Playground

Tower Hamlets London E1

Established by the GLC in 1967 on the site of a former children's hospital, Glamis was closed in 1992 and abandoned. In 2001, it was a derelict ruin overrun by cats but reopened in 2002 under a local management committee.

Now run by local parents, structures have been built in consultation with the kids. To stimulate users' imagination, a bare wooden framework was erected by Hackney Play Association as an "inclusive" walkway enabling children in wheelchairs to take part. Children have since changed it beyond recognition; a garden, huts, wood store and bright paint all contribute to the play environment.

Hackney Marsh Adventure Playground

Hackney London E9

Set up in the early 1960s by the GLC, this playground was built on marshland and is surrounded by housing. The existing structures are from the 1990s: kids drew up designs and helped build the playground using recycled timber and telegraph poles.

The site is now run by the Learning Trust.

Hayward Adventure Playground
Islington London N7

Run by Kidsactive, Hayward was established in the mid 1970s, together with Palace Adventure Playground in Fulham, and Lady Allen Adventure Playground in Wandsworth.

The playground is set in Market Road Gardens, as was a scene from Samuel Beckett's first novel *Murphy*. Like all the Kidsactive sites Hayward has some great structures for disabled children and is well landscaped. Pictured is a hexagonal swing.

Home Park Adventure Playground
Lewisham London SE26

Home Park is possibly one of the smallest adventure playgrounds in London and is run by the local council. Situated at one end of Home Park, it is believed to have been started in 1970. A fire destroyed the playground in 1988 and it was only re-opened in 1991 once funds had been raised to rebuild it.

Homerton Grove Adventure Playground
Hackney London E9 [p11]

Homerton Grove was set up by local people in the early 1970s on a former bombsite.

Structures are made in consultation with children. There is a unique kids-built bowling alley and a high tower from which children can look out but cannot be seen; the tower also acts as a water feature. Children are also involved with the playground's decoration, including life-size plywood cutouts of the regulars.

More areas and structures are in the works, including a sensory garden and pond. The site building is built from recycled materials, it has solar panels on the roof and is a net exporter to the National Grid.

Honor Oak Adventure Playground

Lewisham London SE4 [pp52–53]

Little is known of this playground's history before 1986 when the current playworker Jumbo was employed by the council to rebuild it from its derelict state. Honor Oak is now one of the largest and most complex of London's playgrounds, featuring tunnels, towers, ramps, the longest Burma bridge in London, unique mobile border swings and a network of catwalks that crisscross the entire site and disappear into gorse bushes.

There are mounds, wild, wooded areas and a wide timber walkway that runs through the middle of the playground. All structures are designed in close consultation with the children who play there.

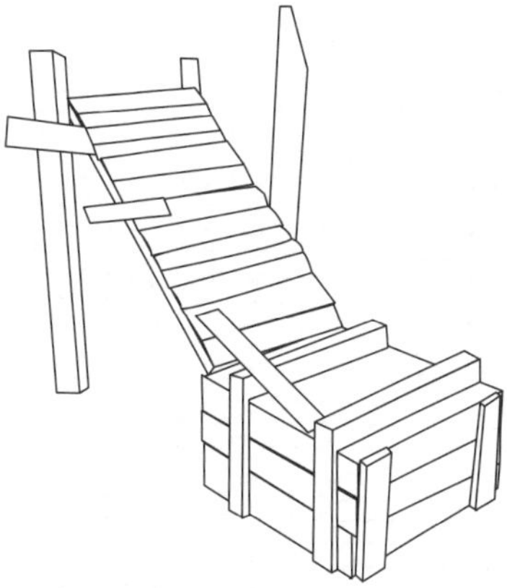

Hornimans Adventure Playground

Kensington & Chelsea London W10 [pp50–51]

Run by local volunteers, Hornimans was started in 1969 on the site of an old coal merchants'. It represents one of the best adventure playgrounds in London, mixing a variety of kids-designed structures together with customised fixed play, all following a chaotic, non-linear design, creating a great deal of choice.

There are many buildings, a central street with camps for girls and boys on either side and a unique earth pizza-oven made by the children.

The playground keeps goats, rabbits, guinea pigs, cats and ducks and there is an environmental pond and garden.

Kennington Play Project
Lambeth London SE5

Little is known of Kennington Park's history but it has been in existence since 1977. Its original prefabricated concrete building still stands but is now used for storage; a new one was built in 1992 and is decorated with murals.

The playground has free-standing stage-like structures and catwalks.

Kimber Road Adventure Playground
Wandsworth London SW18

The playground was started in the late 1970s by local residents with a grant from Wandsworth council, who now run it. Children were closely involved with the construction and design of the early playground but are less so today. The playground was taken over by the council in the early 1990s and the management committee dissolved.

Kimber Road is a bike track/ adventure play hybrid and has, amongst other common playground structures, a large bridge and a multi-level viewing platform/bike rack.

King Henry's Walk Adventure Playground
Islington London N7

[p14]

King Henry's Walk was founded in the early 1970s and is situated on a parade of houses with workshops that were demolished.

Structures are constantly changing and adapted as they fall apart; dens are built around the main parts and there is also a fire pit. Timber has been bought or is donated and on site is an American swing, a Cuban swing and a Baby Rock swing.

The original play building was a very characterful former electricity substation. In 1998 it was demolished and replaced by a purpose built play building.

Lady Allen Adventure Playground

Wandsworth London SW11

Run by Kidsactive, the playground was established in the mid 1970s and is situated in a corner of Wandsworth Common. The playground is named after Lady Allen of Hurtwood, a founding member of Kidsactive and a pioneer of adventure play from the late 1940s who remained active in the field throughout her life.

Lady Allen Adventure Playground is designed primarily for disabled children; it has an extra-wide slide covered in lino for group sliding and ramps that provide wheelchair access to the structures.

Some structures are built to make musical sounds when you interact with them.

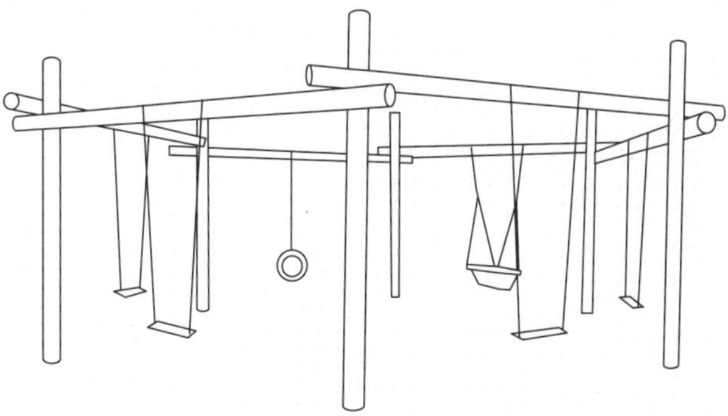

Larkhall Oasis Bike Project

Lambeth London SW8

Larkhall Oasis was established in Larkhall Park in the early 1970s on a former bombsite. Workshops were set up in local primary schools and 28 youth groups were consulted; their ideas were integrated into the designs.

The project consists of a landscaped cycle track and workshops, kart track, a garden and playspace. Future plans involve extending the cycle track across the roofs of the play buildings. A special extra smooth surface is being considered to facilitate rollerblading, skateboarding and remote control cars. There is also camping training in a special wooded area where camps are set up over the weekend.

Leyton Square Adventure Playground
Southwark London SE5

Situated in Leyton Gardens, the playground was set up by Southwark Council, developing from the activities of a mobile council team in a van who set up simple sports facilities in the park or square for an afternoon.

Gradually, permanent structures and indoor facilities were built and in 1990 a fence was erected to mark out the perimeter.

The footballer Rio Ferdinand played here as a boy.

Lollard Street Adventure Playground
Lambeth London SE11

Opened in 1956 on a site that was heavily bombed during the war, Lollard Street is believed to be one of the oldest adventure playgrounds in the country.

Some time before 1977 it moved from its original site, now occupied by the Lillian Baylis School, to a site on the main road that is now used by Ethelred Youth Club.

In 1985 the playground moved again and today it has an extensive system of raised walkways, odd free-standing stage-like structures and a bouncy bridge made from sheets of rubber.

Loughborough Play Project
Lambeth London SW9

Following demolition of housing, Loughborough Play Project was set up in 1973 by the GLC as part of an Amenity Centre incorporating an old people's club, parents and toddlers group and sports centre. Unfortunately, the Amenity Centre closed in the mid 1980s, leaving only the playground and One O'clock Club.

Set within Loughborough Park the playground is dominated by a large mound. There is an extensive network of continuous catwalks and highwalks and murals decorate the playground building.

Lumpy Hill Adventure Playground
Islington London N7

Lumpy Hill was established in 1970 and stands on the site of a former abattoir, part of the larger meat market that occupied the area off Market Street. Next door, over the fence, is Hayward Adventure Playground run by Kidsactive.

Structures are added to and removed yearly.

Marble Hill Adventure Playground
Richmond London TW1 [p13]

It is unclear when Marble Hill Playground was started but given that it was set up by the GLC, a date of 1975 seems probable.

Set in the grounds of Marble Hill House, which at the time was run by the GLC, the House and grounds were handed over to English Heritage after the GLC was abolished. Management of the playground was assumed by the council in 2001, and was subsequently taken over by the voluntary sector, although the council contributes to its upkeep.

Structures are changed in consultation with the kids, and a swing that can accommodate disabled children has recently been built.

Martin Luther King Adventure Playground
Islington London N7

The Martin Luther King Adventure Playground was set up in 1968 after the activist's death.
A management committee was formed by local residents and parents from one of the trusts that were available after his assassination.

Recently all the older structures were removed and only the tower remained when visited. New structures were being built as the book went to press.

Max Roach Play Project
Lambeth London SW9

Established in 1983 by the local council, the playground has many mature trees, a sensory garden, a bog, a purpose-built log cabin, a tower with walkways branching out from it and a small garden house that has been designed after the Maori House at Clandon Park.

Formerly Angel Park, the playground was renamed after the jazz musician Max Roach whose photo is hanging in the hallway of the main hut.

Notting Hill Adventure Playground
Kensington & Chelsea London W10

This exemplary playground was founded in 1958 as part of a positive move towards rebuilding the community after race riots in the area.

In November 2001 the adventure play structures were removed and replaced with new fixed play structures that were built as part of a corporate "team building" day. The new structures are less popular.

Palace Adventure Playground
Hammersmith & Fulham London SW6 [p13]

Palace, run by Kidsactive, is located in the gardens of Fulham Palace and was built on the site of the old palace moat. One of the sluice gates still exists. The playground is landscaped around a building with a distinctive sloping roof. In 2003 there was a tower with a 'Stop The War' banner flying from it.

As at all of the Kidsactive playgrounds, homemade musical instruments, such as xylophones, drums and percussion-type ensembles, made from plastic tubing and pipes, can be found around the playground.

Peckham Rye Adventure Playground
Southwark London SE15

Peckham Rye is believed to have been started in the 1960s by Southwark council. Like Leyton Square, it began as a site on which a mobile team in a van would set up temporary sports facilities during the day.

Ropes were tied to trees for climbing and swinging and these slowly became fixed features of the park; new structures continue to be added.

Plumstead Adventure Playcentre
Greenwich London SE10

Established in the late 1960s, the playground was built on a former quarry and dump site. The design of the playground, conceived in consultation with children, is a continuous raised circuit, enabling users to stay off the ground until they leave.

Whereas the cost of materials has meant that there is now less new design and rebuilding in many playgrounds, the structures here are in constant flux.

The circuit includes small beginners swings at the start, progressing to a challenging Round the World at the end.

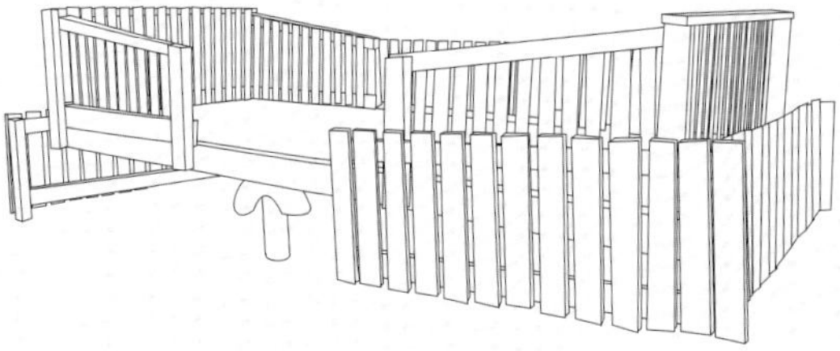

clockwise from left tower, general view, walkway, earth pizza-oven, Hornimans [p43]

clockwise from left tower, walkways and Burma bridge, catwalk, Burma bridge, Honor Oak [p43]

clockwise from above left music stage, platform, general views, Shakespeare Walk [p57]

Rockingham Estate Play Association

Southwark London SE1 [p11]

The playground has occupied a former bombsite since the late 1970s. The foundations of old houses are still visible around the edges of the playground. It has recently been redesigned and landscaped by Handmade Spaces in consultation with children; changes and adaptations are ongoing.

There is an unusual structure designed by a playworker that acts as a series of seats but doubles up as martial arts training apparatus.

Also onsite is a unique communication system that consists of tubes that run under the playground and surface at various locations, allowing people to talk or listen to someone at the other end of the playground.

Gardening is popular at the playground and there is a composting station for the local area.

St. John's Wood Adventure Playground

Westminster London NW8

In 1957 the first lease was signed for this neatly maintained playground, with Lady Allen of Hurtwood as one of the initial signatories.

Built on former terraced houses that were knocked down to make the existing housing estate the site was meant to be a nursery but became an adventure playground instead.

Children were part of initial design and planning; as often happens, the new structures are copies of the old ones they replaced.

Sands End Adventure Playground

Hammersmith & Fulham London SW6

Started in the early 1970s on the site of the old Sunlight Laundry the playground is situated in Langford Park which was renovated along with the playground 15 years ago. There is a small input from children in terms of building and design of the playground.

Shakespeare Walk Adventure Playground

Hackney London N16 [pp54–55]

This inspirational playground was founded in 1976 on a bombsite after local residents squatted the site. Materials for building are scavenged and scrounged. There is a a fire pit and a secret camp area where children are left to build on their own.

The site, like many of London's adventure playgrounds, sits on the border of intense gentrification, giving it a broad social mix. The combination of open access and children's active involvement in playgrounds like Shakespeare's Walk encourages greater multicultural interaction than at traditional playgrounds where interaction is less fundamental.

Shoreditch Playpark

Hackney London N1

Located in Shoreditch Park the playground was established in the late 1970s and occupies a former bombsite. Unique to the playground is a large earthwork snake, part of which acts as a large mound to hide part of the playground. The snake can only be seen properly from the air.

Children make models of structures in balsa wood and card that are then built for real. Onsite are an American swing, a border swing, a tower and a Flying Fox rip slide.

Slade Gardens Adventure Playground

Lambeth London SW9 [p28]

Started in the early 1970s by the local council on a former bombsite, the playground is now run by a management committee of local residents.

Some structures have been in use for 25 years. One tower has an attic space built into its roof and new structures are being built, including one of the highest swings in London, designed and built by Adventure Playground Engineers (APES), who have been building playgrounds in close consultation with children since 2002.

Slade Gardens won the 2003 Adventure Playground of the Year award.

Somerville Adventure Playground

Lewisham London SE14

Somerville was started in 1971 by Ron Martin, whose four children had nowhere to play. Together they took over a bombsite and began slowly building structures. The first hut was a large wooden tea chest which was later replaced by a portacabin with funding from London Adventure Play Association (LAPA).

Hanneke, the playworker here since the late 1970s, is an integral member of the local community. With only a limited budget the playground still changes yearly. There is a slide that can accommodate 25 children at a time. According to Hanneke, the structures that involve the most group interaction are the most popular.

Spa Road Junior Playground
Southwark London SE16

Spa Road, originally called Bermondsey Adventure Playground, was set up by local residents in the 1970s and was handed over to the local council in 1993.

It is quite a sparse playground, surrounded by empty lots in a quiet part of Bermondsey relatively untouched by recent property speculation.

Streatham Vale Play Project
Lambeth London SW16

Streatham Vale was opened in the 1970s as a seasonal playcentre open from April to September. In 1978 the Lambeth Travellers caravan site was established next door and Streatham Vale became a permanent playground, allowing young people from the local community and from the travellers' site to play together all year round.

The playground has an extensive system of walkways and two towers that are capped with square pitched roofs. The smaller tower has a fireman's pole inside.

Three Corners Adventure Playground
Islington London N1

Situated in a large crater-like hole in the middle of some of the most sought-after property in London, Three Corners is ringed by an iron fence and has the disused cells and corridors of the old Clink Prison running below it. The structures are built and designed with the help of the children.

Timbuktu Adventure Playground
Islington London N19

Since the early 1980s Timbuktu has occupied the site of a former factory.

In 2001 all the old structures were removed and a model workshop, run by Hackney Play Association, was held so that children could design and visualise the new playground. The structures have been designed so that kids can get around without touching the ground.

Toffee Park Adventure Playground
Islington London EC1

In 1975 the playground was established as a charity set up by City University students after seeing many kids use the former bombsite as a playground.

The play building was originally a big tin hut; it was replaced in 1989 by a Norwegian log-house. Structures are designed and made with the help of kids and have changed about five times in the past ten years.

Tulse Hill Adventure Playground
Lambeth London SW2

This award-winning playground was founded in 1972 by the GLC on former allotment gardens. Its new building will be developed into a youth and play project.

Structures have been built in consultation with the children that use them; these include slides, walkways, swings, a sand pit and nature garden.

It is thought locally that a river runs underneath the site.

Waterside Play and Youth Project

Islington London N1

Set up in the early 1970s, the playground sits on a former bed factory that was burnt down by local kids. In keeping with tradition, the playground itself was also burnt down some years back. Hole digging is enjoyed and they are still excavating old bed frames and springs.

The playground's design has been developed in consultation with the children. They grow their own fruit and veg on site, there is a fire pit, space for building camps, an American swing, two border swings and two smaller swings.

Weavers Adventure Playground

Tower Hamlets London E2 [pp10, 16]

Started up by a group of parents on bombed weavers' cottages and officially opened in 1975, the playworker Tracy Salmon played here as a child. Like many of the best playgrounds, Weavers' spirit has been helped by continuity of staffing.

The structures are kids-built and constantly changing. Timber is scavenged and donated and they still collect junk for building. Until 1990 the playground was also a city farm. At one time it was famous for its TV-themed structures and sculptures and Brian Cant from the children's TV programme *Playaway* made a VIP guest visit.

White Horse Road Adventure Playground

Tower Hamlets London E1

Built in 1974 on an old bombsite the playground was set up by local parents and children. During school holidays children would build small corrugated tin structures but now there is nothing left that was built by children.

Willington Road Adventure Playground
Lambeth London SW9

Willington Road was set up around 1979 and had a small portable building made from shipping containers. The playground was one of a number of new provisions identified by the development officer of the council's children's play section at that time.

The playground moved from its original location further up the same street to a site it shares with Pyramid Youth Club; together they were developed in 1988 by ILEA Youth Service, supported with funding from the Inner City Partnership. The playground is now the base for the Lambeth Youth Steel Band.

Woolwich Adventure Playcentre
Greenwich London SE18

On a thin stretch of land between the railway and Woolwich Church Street this playground, set up in the early 1980s, has had a no-build ban for many years, with few structures remaining.

York Gardens Adventure Playground
Wandsworth London SW11

York Gardens began life in 1978 as St. John's Adventure Playground near St. John's Hospital, Wandsworth, on a derelict site that was taken over by local children and parents. A year later the council was ready to redevelop the site and the playground moved to York Gardens. The council paid for staff to help run it while a management committee raised funds for maintenance and running costs; the council took over after the management committee folded.

The original structures were kids-built. Today there is an aerial slide and a large two-tiered rampway/tower.

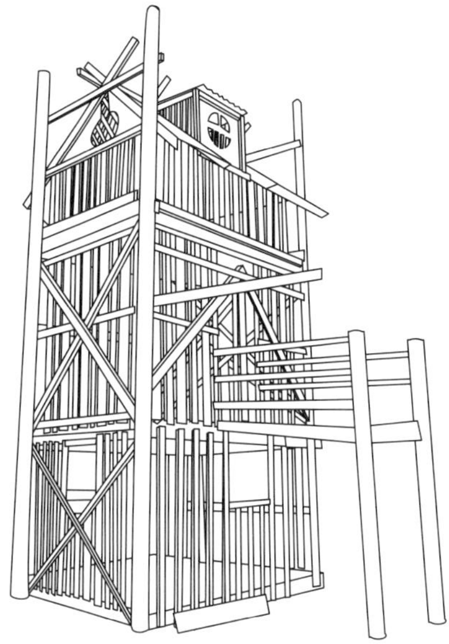

Thanks

This book is a brief introduction to the world of adventure play, focusing for practical reasons on London. The project began as an idea to make an exhibition about the city's adventure playgrounds, primarily their history, design and architecture. I began searching for an archive or a comprehensive record of adventure play in London but the closest I got was a shoe box full of unsorted and uncredited photos. I realised then that I would have to immerse myself deeper and begin my own documentation. I decided to visit the adventure playgrounds listed on London Play's website, photographing the structures, interviewing playworkers and researching each playground's history. The more playgrounds I visited, the longer the list of people to contact grew; this process ended up taking two years, slowly connecting up the playgrounds and the network of people across London. The result is not a comprehensive, but a representative survey of London's adventure playgrounds.

I would like to thank Hanneke at Somerville, Jumbo at Honor Oak and Barry at the Dumps, Rita at Slade Gardens, Haley at Evergreen, Andrea at Toffee Park and Darrius at Barnard Park, Gary Martin at Southwark Council, Peter McNally at Lambeth Council, Mark Halden at Watford Council, Jess Milne and Mick Conway at Hackney Play Association, Nick Jackson at Islington Play Association, Dave Perkins at Kidsactive, Adrian Voce, Anne McLaughlin and Sue Coates at London Play. Thanks also to Janet Dalglish, Alan Sutton, Sandra Melville, Terry Moore, Stephen Derby, Tracey Salmon, Ricardo Guichard and Alma Pirie, Barbara Wedderburn, Claudette Barnes, Rita Dyer, Peter Leandry, David Quaye, Jenny O'Shea, Tessa Martin, and all the other playworkers and line managers who I spoke to over the phone or met but whose names I never knew. During my research some playgrounds on the list closed or removed their structures before I could photograph them and in some cases the playworkers had moved on. Glamis Road in Shadwell has successfully re-opened and is included in the book.

I would especially like to thank Emily Pethick, Tim Barnes, Paul Claydon, Keith Cranwell, Richard Embray, Cecilia Bonilla, Elinor Jansz, Alex Sainsbury, Grant Lambie, Jess Milne, Marta Nowicka, Ian Hunt, Stephan Dillemuth, Tue Grenfort, Jakob Jakobsen, Charlotte Rylance, Liana Sperow, and Eva and Roger Heyes.

Nils Norman, November 2003

The Rec, Ripon Street, Sheffield, 1972 photo: Jess Milne